POEMS
FOR
PATRIOTS

POEMS
FOR
PATRIOTS

AERUM DELEVAN

authorHOUSE®

AuthorHouse™
1663 Liberty Drive
Bloomington, IN 47403
www.authorhouse.com
Phone: 1-800-839-8640

First published by AuthorHouse   09/24/2011

ISBN: 978-1-4670-3898-0 (sc)
ISBN: 978-1-4670-3897-3 (ebk)

Library of Congress Control Number: 2011917285

Printed in the United States of America

ACKNOWLEDGEMENTS

Many thanks to Max and Deborah Quayle, Jeanette Smolnik,

and Sally Delevan for editing this work.

Much gratitude, also, to my supportive family and to this great country,

which allows each of us to freely express the things we hold so dear,

in whatsoever medium we choose.

POEMS FOR PATRIOTS

These words were inspired. I pray that they will bring hope, courage, and understanding to all those who share my love for my Creator and for my country, the greatest land of all, the United States of America.

Our country was not founded easily, but through the shedding of much blood, and through the sacrifices of brave souls who sought to bring about and to preserve our freedom.

This compilation of poems celebrates our Founders—courageous men whose ideals gave us the foundation upon which we continue to build—one that has brought us through wars and conflicts, good times, and bad. These poems also celebrate all of those great heroes who have fought, and many times died, to preserve and protect that Constitutional foundation upon which our country is based.

May God continue to bless this grand and glorious country. I am, and ever will be, proud to be an American.

Aerum A. Delevan

SECTION ONE:

AMERICANREVOLUTION

1776

Grown men grew bold
And fought tyranny's hold;
They were brave men fighting in the snowy cold.
Not soldiers, but just volunteers,
They had neither experience nor Army careers.
They did have courage; that was never in lack;
They followed their leaders and never did slack.
Just simple farmers, people like you;
But they had a dream, which they wanted, and knew.
One simple word, that's all it was,
And for it they'd die, because,
Freedom is as freedom does.

HELL'S FIRE

Battles fought for freedom's sake:
Patriots die within the wake.
For tyranny's grip it came about,
'Cause men of passion arose to flout.

For freedom's song rang loud and strong;
Patriots rallied to fight the throng.
Into hell's fire, they marched on,
In order to right the greatest wrong.

With angel's protection they hoped to dare,
Overcoming every trial set to ensnare.
At night could be heard many a patriot's prayer
But, never one as great as the man's★ on the white mare.
With divine Providence, there was no despair'
For, Washington knew that God did care
About this country, that couldn't compare.

And now, my friends, will you go there
And find the courage to stare down the evil, in this country
so fair?
It's now up to us to repair America, for whom we lovingly
care.

★ General George Washington

— *Aerum Delevan* —

LINES OF RED

Up Breed's Hill the British came
And musket balls fell, like rain.
The lines of red came, without fear, they said,
As they marched past, their wounded and dead.

The militia men fired into that line of red,
But, as the battle waged on, they began to dread—
Was there no end to that line of red?
So, to their commanders they said,
"We keep killing these men in red,
But, they outnumber us so, let us retreat, instead."

The day was lost, but the battle was won,
For it was the British who lost quite a sum.

After this, the brave men said, "They're not invincible, these
lines of red."
No more fear, no more dread,
With courage, they defeated those lines of red.
So those who died, and those who bled, saved us from
tyranny's spread.

FREEDOM

Men of hope,
Men of faith,
Men who fought for freedom's grace,
They were men from ever place.
Believing in the cause,
They faced the enemies of God's disgrace.
No food, no shoes, they were all displaced,
But still it was hope that that they embraced.
For their freedom was the thing at stake,
In this land, to be, the United States.

— Aerum Delevan —

THE REGULARS

The rifles all shone, one early morn,

As those on the field all mocked with scorn.

These men were peasants, trying to fight the crown;

How could they be so foolish, so futile, for none had
renown.

Farmers, smithies, and woodsmen, all average men,

Dared dream of a country where men could be free, so war
would begin.

So, into the fray, all went they;

Future generations would proudly say

They were patriots who had won the day.

The muskets roared and the drums were heard,

And these average men charged, at their captains' words.

The war was won, though many a tear

Was shed for those patriots, who died through those years.

Now the Stars and the Stripes and Don't Tread on Me

Can hang proudly o'er, this land of liberty.

TATTERED AND WORN

In disarray they marched into the battlefield's view
As cannons and muskets fired, penetrating flesh and sinew.
The British charged, with bayonets bare
As most of the men wondered why they were there.
British officers stood to stare
At farmers, not soldiers—how unfair.

Volunteers, true, went to fight for the cause,
To prevent unjust rule and welcome just laws.
A few honorable traits these common men shared;
They all wanted freedom, so bravely would bare,
A heavy burden, to forge a nation of care.

Raggedy men in tattered clothes,
Made a great stand, while the British imposed.
In the end, a new nation was formed,
Thanks to brave men—the tattered and worn.

— Aerum Delevan —

SECTION 2:

CIVIL WAR

A NATION DIVIDED

Incorrigible practices brought widespread scorn.
A nation not yet born was divided and torn;
The stars and the stripes versus the stars and the bars,
Men would bleed from near and from far.

The boys in blue were Yankees, true.
And the men who wore gray would always say,
They were "Johnny's" and proud to fight, for nothing could sway,
As Robert E. Lee led the Confederacy;
Ulysses S Grant, a Union man, found himself on Lincoln's right hand.

So, the two sides would clash and, after a long bloody bash,
The war came to a close, at long last.
Once silence came to battle grounds still and cold,
All of those men, so brave and so bold,
Returned to their homes, after proudly breaking slavery's dark hold.

Our country was preserved;
But, did they get what they deserved?
Our country is now again divided and torn
By the shrouded cloak of a communist thorn.
So, who, now, is brave enough to blow a warning horn?

THE YEARS THAT WERE FIVE

A country was divided.
A country was torn.
So, old honest Abe said, "We can no longer ignore."

A spark was lit and the cannons roared,
In this greatest battle, our Civil War.
It was all about rights, the right to be free,
They fought and they died to ensure liberty.

How could Abe know what was in store?
The blue and the gray embroiled in the grizzliest war;
The soldiers all struggled just to survive,
But freedom would o'er come in the years that were five.

— Aerum Delevan —

SLAVERY THEN AND NOW

States rights, what are they worth?

How about blood, and how about earth.

History is something that runs in the veins;

Muskets spewed forth lead, yet those brave mens' memories
remained.

The Civil War tore families apart;

Many wondered why the war had to start.

The Blue and the Grey, brave men, all, were they;

But, slavery's depravity helped the North win the day.

Slavery, even now?

Are you kidding! Just how?

Modern day slavery, you say, isn't much of a sin;

But, many an American, similar shackles are in.

If you don't see, then I'll explain it to thee;

Slavery is DEBT, you see.

Credit cards and spending make all of us slaves;

If Lincoln could see us, he'd be turning in his grave.

So, don't be like the Blue and the Gray,

By letting modern day slavery have its echoing way.

SECTION 3:

WORLD WAR I

THE GREAT WAR

The Great War, World War One,
Started like so many others, with the firing of a gun;
Then a prince lay dead in the street,
And many men marched with thunderous feet.

The Kaiser was our enemy; in the trenches he lay,
With machine guns, artillery, and a deadly aerial display.
Millions lay dead in heaps on the earth,
While their spirits marched on, into heaven's great birth.

The Great War ended, as Wilson★ declared,
But only for a short time, would the world be spared.
A quarter century later, to our great chagrin,
World War II would lure us in.

★ Woodrow Wilson—28th President of the United States

THIRTEEN REASONS

In the First World War, Germans went about to settle a
score,
But when violence started, it escalated, more.
Into the trenches those men went, dying from wounds and
disease,
As the people in power still did as they pleased.

When the war spilled over into France's back yard,
President Wilson decided, that was too far.
For the thirteen reasons that passed his front desk,
He sent Americans into those hellish trenches, just to
thump his great chest.

Millions would die, shedding their blood,
Their bodies rescued from lying in the mud.
And, after the war, just what happened then?
A new war started, and men killed again.

— *Aerum Delevan* —

NO MAN'S LAND

In those muddy trenches of World War One,
The men felt safe from the German's gun;
But when the whistle blew, it was then they did know,
They were about to cross over the devil's plateau.

Bullets flew as shells rained down on the heads
Of those brave young men, who soon would be dead.
That place bears the name, "No Man's Land,"
A suitable name, for it truly was God damned.

Nothing lived long in that hell on earth;
Any survivor was blessed as one of great worth.

SECTION 4:

WORLD WAR II

ENEMIES ON ALL SIDES

The gears of an evil machine,
Otherwise was known as the Nazi regime.
A mechanized army that was so strong,
It would consume all of Europe, before long.

Across the ocean, a fleet slowly steamed
Toward a small island, that lazily dreamed.
Thunderous blasts were heard one lazy Sunday morn,
And the peaceful bliss was shattered by the screaming air
raid horns.
With nowhere to run and nowhere to hide,
America's great fleet sank, indenting her pride.
The dreadful attack in infamy remains,
Awakening America again to war, what a shame.

The Nazis from the East, Japan from the West,
Surrounded America, so at her behest,
Brave men charged into the enemies nest.
Many would die, but heroes were born;
In the end, the victors' crowns would adorn.

GOOD MEN

Why is it that good men go,
Taken from us, violently so?
What did they do to deserve such a fate,
While leaving behind something so great?
Family and friends are now all in grief,
And praying to the Lord for a little relief.

This life is so precious, be that as it may,
Take care of yourself; never go astray.
For it's a fact, we'll all die one day.
So live each day for your brothers, and then God will say,
"Enter into my fold, for you did obey."

— *Aerum Delevan* —

D-DAY

The land was dark!
The clouds were gray!
Some of the men would kneel and would pray.
They thanked their maker for their life,
And yearned to survive the unending strife.

The guns rang loud; the bullets sang their deadly song,
But 'twas on the beach that things went so wrong.
The bunkers were charged, but all was in vain,
For the enemy came there to kill; they came there to maim.

The few now remaining mustered courage again,
Overcoming all odds, what spectacular men!
For freedom they were fighting; they knew the way,
And victory was theirs on that *glorious* D-Day.

SECTION 5:

KOREAN WAR

LAND OF THE MORNING CALM

Time reverts back, like flipping a page,
A time of blood, bullets, and incredible rage.
Things weren't so peaceful in the land of the morning calm,
Because, right at this time, the battle was going all wrong.
The lieutenant ordered his men, "Retreat!"
The men ignored him; he shouted louder, in repeat.
All his men died; it was a total defeat.

The lieutenant was the only one standing; he was all alone,
So, from the battlefield, he flew safely home.
He was a man of honor; his name was Harry Ray.
To me, he was grandpa; that's all I'll say.
His battle was over, the war so far away,
But the war's now on our shores, in the heart of the USA.
No bullets, no bombs, but ideals now clash.
Freedom or oppression, which one do YOU think will last?

INCHON

In Korea's southern Port of Pusan, despair was felt, but the
soldiers pressed on;

Mac Arthur boldly landed at Inchon.

When all seemed lost, hope was restored;

The armies of the North retreated and whirled,

For now they were surrounded by Allied might unfurled.

Soon after the landing at Inchon,

Soul was retaken, and a nation lived on.

THOSE WHO REMAIN

Young men thought that war might be fun,
Then found themselves facing Communist guns.
Though they fought bravely, the battle grew sore;
But valiant obedience would help a nation restore.

The same ground was lost, then re-gained,
But the cost of lives ever mounted, as the battle waned.
Victory seemed close, 'til China stretched out her red hand;
The soldiers were overwhelmed by the numerous band.

Mac Arthur, fearing the worst,
Was retired by Truman, and the war grew worse.
Our soldiers, feeling abandoned by our own,
Just wanted the war to end, so they all could go home.

Eisenhower won a mighty campaign,
Putting an end to the fighting, though some do remain.

REMEMBER ME

There was a war in forty and nine
On a small peninsula that was divine.
One day there came a threat from above,
And gripped those in the South, like a dark-yielded glove.
Fear was felt throughout the world;
'til America's might was unfurled.
The red, white, and blue went to support the yin and the
yang,
As our soldiers marched, they sang.

We are a nation, who defends those that are weak,
To protect their freedoms, and the liberty they seek.

The war was going well, though our men faced pure hell.
Then the Chinese pushed our men back,
Showing us, just where we did lack.

We lost too much ground, and our public finally found
That the war had ended, without so much as a sound.
We left the peninsula in the East China Sea,
But the men who fought there still whisper,
"Do they still remember me?"

— *Aerum Delevan* —

SECTION 6:

VIETNAM

REVERIE

Not even a breath escapes my lips;
Nervous tension builds, as my sweat rolls and drips.
The jungle canvas is just over me,
I look up for the blue, of what little I can see.

From my mind escapes a prayer.
Should I get on my knees? No, I was already there.
Then the sergeant barked; I snapped out of my reverie;
I raised my head in time to see,
Hell wide open, unleashing her fury.

Soon I was surrounded by the dying and dead;
Everything went black; a bullet struck my head.
A flash of white light revealed long lost family and friends;
Amazed, I now realized that life never ends.

I wanted to stay with them but they told me, "No;"
They said I had more work to do, down below.
So with ringing in my head, like a great gong,
I awoke in a field hospital, in the middle of 'nam.

THE DIVINE

The honor was ours; your words were divine,
Giving us this land, in this our time.
The people who served, our freedom preserved,
And a nation was reserved, for a flag that they so proudly
served.

Over the course of a century good men stood proud;
They all saluted as others were enveloped by its comforting
shroud.
White boxes were on display, cradling the remains
Of the good soldiers, whose lives they gave.

Taps were played, as caskets were lowered into the graves,
And the flag was raised to half mast on those days.
Old Glory was folded with such great care,
And reverently presented to loved ones, there.

— Aerum Delevan —

WHAT WAS IT FOR?

Red streams ran free
Under the jungle's lush canopy,
And sounds of wounded, from amongst the dead,
Were heard crying for this horrible nightmare to end.

Then came distant sounds of thunderous blades,
Alerting the troops that help was on its way.
But there were too many men for the choppers to carry;
Some courageously gave up their rides for the weary.

And somewhere in that hellish nightmare,
The flame of hope was still lit, for the soldiers did care;
For, though they all saw combat's hellish dark side,
None denied that God was on their side.

So, when all of the battles came to a close,
Just what was it all for?
No one really knows.

TO MY DAD

As I think and as I pray,
I remember the things *you* used to say.
A patriot you are, both brave and true,
So, with love, this poem, I dedicate to you.

I am your son, though weak and frail;
I still do ponder when you told your tale,
About your friends that blazed that trail.
In the jungle deep, the terror spread,
For in the night came fear and dread,
And when the dawn came you'd count the dead;
In your heart you hoped and plead
That your friends weren't amongst the dead.
But to your sorrow, and to your despair,
All of your friends were tragically there.

Now they are gone and time has slowly moved on,
But, in your memory, they still live on.
Upon that endless wall of black stone,
Are all of the names of the people you've known.

And so you weep as you stare, wishing your name, not
theirs, was there.
But now, this is hard, because I care, for all of those whom
God did spare.

— *Aerum Delevan* —

THE WALL

A wall that is black, a wall of cold stone,
Just as cold as those names that it holds.
Those names of brave men, who have gone to the grave,
And, for some reason, into villains were made.

Most were just kids, no more than nineteen,
Yet, they fought in battles that were ever so frightening.
They marched into jungles in a land far away,
But back at home, just killers were they.
My father and my uncle were also there,
But, how many of you *really* did care?

I know they are all heroes; I know this to be true,
For many fought to their death for the Red, White, and
Blue.
So, why were they mocked? Who knows!
I don't have the answer, probably never will;
But, that wall of black stone will forever cause chills.
It holds not just the names of those who have died,
But, this is where their memories reside.

SECTION 7:

9/11/01

REMEMBER

Do you remember that day,
When the two towers fell, and you knelt quickly to pray?
Just as a great epitaph,
The dust rolled on out with the draft.
New York's horizon fair
Lost its luster, along with the pair.
Close to three thousand precious lives lost,
How can we bear this horrible cost!

Now just a hole graces that place,
Like the one in our heart, as tears roll down our face.
Now, let us exclaim, "This is not our disgrace!"
But, vengeance and anger let us replace,
With our most solemn fortitude, and quickly make hast,
To rebuilt that most sacred place.

We now humbly place our hearts and souls into His grace.
And, let us all pray, He will now say,
"I will bless the USA."

BLACK SNOW

Early morning in New York fair
Loomed two towers above the busy square;
Then all the people stopped to stare,
For those two towers where no longer there.

Above New York the smoke now loomed,
But just before New Yorkers heard the boom,
They saw a spectacle in the sky,
And could not believe their eyes.

The planes were too low; the fear started to grow,
And, like a bad horror show,
The world that we all know
Fell apart like a black snow.

So now an empty lot is there,
And some are saying that they don't care.
But what of the families and friends,
I dare to ask; why is there a great hole there?
Can we not honor them by rebuilding once again?
For we are Americans, you see, and we will honor those
who keep us free.

— *Aerum Delevan* —

TOWERS

The two towers stood above the world;
In their shadows, the people's lives swirled.
Below, the streets of New York were twirled,
As, within the towers, people traded throughout the world.

Then one morning a plot was unfurled
That made Americans' hearts to curl;
September eleventh, the hijackers came;
They stole the planes, then made everything change.

These terrorists were using God's name
To start a war with us, they claim.
But, I say that it's a shame
That all of those people died in vain,
For, have we forgotten from whence we came?
It isn't our government that we should blame,
But "in God we trust" is where we must remain.

TOWERS TWO

The sun shone through the towers two,
And burned away Central Park's dew.
No one knew when those planes flew
Exactly what would ensue.

One by one the scrapers fell,
And engulfed New York like the gates of hell.
And on Liberty's Island, where she does dwell,
The black fog from the towers encased her like a shell.

The terrorists had kicked in America's front porch,
But when the fog cleared, Liberty still clung to her torch.
Now the giant's great eyes did slowly wake
To the horrifying blasts that the planes did create.

Cries from the city rang loud in the giant's great head
As the giant bellowed, "These terrorists will soon be dead!"
So, New York, we remember you still,
And that great hole, that no one did fill.
America, you must swallow your pill,
And all your promises, you must fulfill.

— Aerum Delevan —

SECTION 8:

IRAQ AND AFGHANISTAN

DESERT SAND

In the desert sands known as Iraq and Afghanistan,
There are brave Americans attempting to free these two
lands.
So, I plead, please give them a helping hand.

Though they may be far from home,
Yet, in our hearts they are known,
For they have all shown, that American courage is still sown.

So, let us all now pray
For their safe return home, someday.
Then we can all say,
"I've done my part today."

So, soldiers, hold your heads up high,
And people will whisper as you pass by
Because they cannot deny
That you are all heroes, by and by.

DESERT PLAY

A great wind blows and sand stings your eyes,
All the while you're squinting into the darkness inside.
Your heart is pounding in your chest,
But you know you're braver than all the rest.

Swallowing hard, the fear subsides;
And, in a moment, you realize,
You now have entered that killing zone,
Knowing, it may not lead to home.

The sound, of guns blazing, rings in your ears,
But you just stay alive, despite all your fears.
The adrenalin falls; the battle is won,
Then, soon arises, that great desert sun.

The night has ended; the morning has come,
Exhausted, your day is finally done.
The rest of the day you sleep away;
Counting the days, 'til you can truly say,
"Good bye," to this dreadful desert play.

— *Aerum Delevan* —

SOLDIER

I'm not a soldier, but to those who are,
Know that we care about you, though you're fighting afar.
For each of the soldiers in Iraq and Afghanistan,
Know that your country is proud of each woman and man;
For, I know that I am!

You left your families and all of your friends,
To go to battle, America's peace to defend.
So, I promise, you'll never be forgotten, my friends,
And will return with honor, and none will contend.

GUARDIANS

The guardians are with you,
Although you may not see;
In the field they watch o'er you,
And send the Lord your plea.

Though the desert sand may sting you,
And may parch you dry,
Just remember that you have angels,
Who are always standing by.

Though the shadows bind you, in the dark of night,
His hand is on your shoulder, as you go into the fight.
So, if you start to think all hope is gone,
Just know that guardian angels are singing a battle song,
For your family is praying that you'll be safe from harm.

When you return home, with your head held high,
You'll realize that what I said was true,
That the guardians were watching over you,
In those sands that are so dry.

— Aerum Delevan —

SECTION 9:

POEMS FOR PATRIOTS

EVER END

One nation, under God, for this land is where good men
trod.

They all came here to be free, to create a land of liberty.

First was Columbus, who made a journey bold,

Then there were the pilgrims, in the days of old;

They wanted freedom to worship, so escaped from tyranny's
hold

In three ships of a Spanish mold.

The ships' names went down in history

As the Nina, the Pinta, and the Santa Maria.

Then more came, though not as extravagantly;

All wanted one thing—freedom without hypocrisy.

Next a war brewed, as the new land stewed, but it wasn't for
food.

The English and French divided the land;

As casualties mounted, they were buried in the sand.

But this bloody battle wouldn't be the last,

For this war would act as a catalyst, fast.

A new war broke out and freedom sprang true,

As freemen defeated the English; who knew?

A new nation soon gathered under the red, white, and blue.

Alas, this land would still see more, as people died in a great Civil War.

Will this ever end? Will peace not begin?

No, not until the end of man's sin.

AWAKEN!

America is blest, above all the rest,
But now we face our darkest test.
What exactly happened? Why have we strayed?
Do we not recognize that God is the way?

Warnings from some patriots fell on deaf ears,
So, are we happy, now that Liberty's in tears?
How much longer will we let this go on?
Do we even know the old patriots' songs?
America the Beautiful—The Star Spangled Banner, too—
Just what have your teachers been teaching to you?
What about the Pledge of Allegiance to the Red, White,
and Blue?
But now, it's apparently all true; there are people out there
who'd rather sue.

Whatever happened to American pride?
I wonder if, in the eighties, it died.
Remember, when that red wall came crashing down,
Some, in the shadows, sought to recover the crown.
Slowly they infected our country of peace,
And, now, we ask, "Why has liberty ceased?"

THE CAUSE IS GREAT

The greatest generation has passed and gone,
And now the flower children march progressively on.
In the darkest hour, we struggle to fight the power.
With words of truth, we bring light, with proof,
So, fellow Americans, we can no longer be aloof.

The cause is great,
So, now, all awake!
Else it will be God who will us forsake,
And drive us off this land that he did make.
This land that's free from all tyranny,
A place that we all call home, you see.
America is where all are free:
At least that is how it *should* be.

— *Aerum Delevan* —

THE PATRIOT

What makes patriots, patriots?

What makes heroes, heroes?

Is it something they say?

Or something they do?

I think it comes from something deep inside, don't you?

Patriots and heroes aren't born, they're raised,

With ethics, and morality, and a virtuous gaze.

You can tell who they are from a single glance,

For, there's something in their eyes, put there, not by chance.

For not all patriots nor heroes on a battlefield are found,

For, if you truly look, they are all around.

They may be neighbors, or friends, or even from your family descend;

Made like a clay that can be molded and bent,

But, in their hearts is found a strength; it never ends;

And a spirit that truly transcends.

MY COUNTRY

My country is of Thee, that's why I pray to Thee;
So, I thank thee for my country of liberty and beauty.
My God, I pray to thee to tell you I am sorry,
For my country no longer heeds thee;
For corrupt men are insulting me, and trying to take my
liberty.

The founders are weeping
For their writings are withering and losing their meaning.
Our banner was streaming and used to be gleaming;
Why has it lost its meaning?

God, are you listening while we are praying,
For, our freedoms are slowly fading.
People of my country, I now ask of thee,
Don't let our country slip into history
As the one who lost sight of its liberty.

I have this dream you see,
One of my country and how it can, again, be,
Where freedom rings true,
Whether you're Gentile or Jew;
For, no matter who,
God is watching over you.

— Aerum Delevan —

My God, and my friends, I pray
That you will hear my words and say,
"I'm an American you see,
And I truly stand for liberty."

EVERYONE

Listen to me, everyone,
For I am speaking, as my Father's son.
I know you don't know me,
But hear me, I plead,
For all of these words are divine in deed.
I beg you humbly; I plead today,
Just listen to me, then chose to obey.

I love you all, for soon is the fall,
So, a warning I give you, like unto Saul.
I may be humble; I'm not very learned,
But, with these words, I hope you to spur.

You all seem lost, but do not despair,
For I know for a fact that God is there,
And he will listen to your honest prayer.

— Aerum Delevan —

LIBERTY

Great land of liberty,
Corruption has taken over Thee.
In these past years, I see the peoples' fears;
I sit idly by as they wipe their tears
On rags that were flags that used to fly true.
Oh, red, white, and blue, what has happened to you?

Once so great a nation, it's now lost its station.
Patriots of old, we've sold your nation of gold to enemies
cold,
Who have no soul and are taking control;
They're breaking the mold, raping both the young and the
old.

Our freedoms are gone like an old patriot's song;
Where have all the brave men gone?

WARY

The time is here; the time is now.
So watch my friends,
For you'll know how.

For there are wolves among the sheep;
They lay in wait for that time to creep
Into the flock; they lay low,
Telling the people that they aren't so.
But with their fangs they will sear
While the warnings we have failed to hear.

But, my friends we are now awake,
And now is the time to correct our mistake.
We must be watchful! We must be alert!
For there are people who will hurt!
So now be strong and don't desert!

You are needed, so do not shirk,
And pray to God while in your church.
So, when you do your search,
You'll find the truth; then you won't lurch
To that place where tyrants perch.

— Aerum Delevan —

SONS AND DAUGHTERS

Sons and daughters of liberty,
I write about this country that God has given unto thee.
Will you just sit idly by,
And do nothing as your freedoms slowly die?
Or, will you espouse these words three:
Faith, hope, and charity.

Internal corruption and tyranny
Are trying to crush our beloved country.
So, then, who will it be who brings back freedom unto
thee?
Will you now stand with me,
And say, "No!" to corruption's spree?

It's the Founders' desire,
To which I aspire—
That our country will never fall to the cowardly or bold
As long as we, the Constitution, will firmly uphold.

Terrorists will eventually see
That this is God's land, entrusted to those who believe.
They'll know that God inspired the Founders,
And gave them powers to lay the groundwork for these past
hours
To keep this God blessed country ours.

REVOLUTION

There are three things that we all must know.
They are important; this is so.
The times revolve around these three:
War, peace, and revolution, you see.
The times may change, but these three do not,
For we are human, and this is our lot.

But it is important that we chose
Whether we are Gentiles, or with the Jews.
It was Jesus who said, "These are my sheep."
Now, I pray, that you will awaken from your deep sleep.

For time is now marching upon revolution's front door,
So, will you be vigilant? Or chose to ignore?
Silent majority, you need to awaken!
It's the world's freedom that is at stake!

With truth and with boldness, we must defend.
The Declaration and Constitution, which need no amends.
They are our foundation; that's all.
The end.

— *Aerum Delevan* —

PILLAR

History is forgotten; mistakes are doomed to be repeated;
Those in power have no idea how we the people should be treated.
Thank the Founders for their wisdom, for they knew this time would come,
When good becomes evil and everything gets unraveled, and undone.

The Constitution is our pillar; it binds us and defines us.
It guides us individually, and as a nation,
Defining our God given rights to move, as we choose, from station to station.

The Constitution—a document, a paper, with more than just words,
It's an outline, a blueprint, a guide to freedom and courage.
It has strength, brings light, and contains everything dear.
So, has it changed? Has it bent? What is it that I fear?

It's the people that have changed, playing their greedy political games,
But the Constitution remains true, and will forever be the same.

PRAYER

God, are you there?
Are you hearing our payers?

We pray, to You,
That You will sustain our Red, White, and Blue.
Though corruption has spread,
There are people who remember the promises said
When you first came, and died, and bled—
That this will be a nation true,
As long as we just follow You.

— Aerum Delevan —